BLUES DOULA

Poems by Meta Commerse

Story Medicine Worldwide Publications
ASHEVILLE, NORTH CAROLINA

Also by Meta Commerse

Landscapes of Abuse (2001)

Rainsongs: Poems of a Woman's Life (2012)

The Mending Time, a novel (2014)

Womaning, a Memoir (forthcoming)

Diamonds and Pyramids: Story Medicine for Racial Healing (forthcoming)

ⓖ

Copyright © 2019 by **Meta Commerse**

All rights reserved. No part of this publication may be reproduced, distributed or transmitted in any form or by any means, without prior written permission.

Story Medicine Worldwide Publications
P.O. Box 1471
Asheville, N.C. 28802-1471
www.storymedicineworldwide.com

Blues Doula / Meta Commerse. — 1st ed.
ISBN 978-0-578-58769-1

Design & Book Services: Carol Majors, PUBLICATIONS UNLTD, Raleigh, NC *for Shikamana*

CONTENTS

ONE   HOMAGE
Coretta   2
Cissy's 2012 Poem   5
Two Seconds Tender (for Burt Bacharach)   8
Aretha   11
When we Dance (for Sting)   14
Mama Frank   16
The Secret (for Aunt Elaine)   18

TWO   EMOTE
Ode to Brown Baby   22
'71 Love Poem   26
Blues Doula   29
Intersection   32
Umbilicus   34
Lament: Ode to Mother Emmanuel   37
Dark, Darker, Darkest   39
Double Consciousness   41
Say My Name   43
Soil Sorrows   46
Madagascar   50

Three **Home**
  Crone Song *54*
  One (for Mama) *56*
  Hair *59*
  Mama *61*
  Genesis Three Sixteen *63*
  What I Miss *66*
  Black Echoes *70*

ACKNOWLEDGEMENTS

This collected work would be impossible without the help, influence, and love from the following people: Johari Amini, Kim Williams, Haki Madhubuti, Dorothy Watkins, Elesa Commerse, Pamela Plummer, Maria Hamilton Abegunde, Jocelyn DeLay, Pat Johnson, Mahan Siler, Nancy Ackermann Cole, JacKaline Stallings, Dennis Fotinos, Lisa Rowe, Chris Wells, Ellane Chandler, Frances Smith, Elaine Williams, Sarah Skinner and Georgette Matthew. I will be forever grateful to them all.

FOREWORD

> *Sometimes all a prophet can do*
> *is describe what looms*
> *prepare for great dawnings*
> *whisper prayers*
> *into hands rubbed bare*
> *and wait ...*
>   from "Cissy's 2012 Poem"

Or, sometimes all a prophet can do is tell her truth in words that have struggled to scream through her mouth but instead have waited, patiently for decades, for her hand to pick up the pen and chant.

Blues Doula invites you into Meta Commerse's life. If you accept the invitation, you agree to enter a Black woman's herstory: poems about everyday acts and thoughts that witness what make Black life and living painful and joyful... everywhere that Black women live. Most of all, these poems are Meta's witnessing, documenting the transformation and healing of herself through individual and historical traumas, and the struggles to acknowledge how and why they are connected and continual.

In her title poem, "Blues Doula," Meta accomplishes all of this when she invokes the Blues tradition: working the poem to a crescendo that mimics the "lonely rage" of being Black, being woman; the pretense of being all right and the weariness of nothing being right. It's almost as if she is saying, you know what I'm talking about: "Most times I ignored / their urging, / ignored them speaking – / demanding emergence – / pushing their way out. / ... What black woman tears? / So / I smiled instead / denied them, / ... because / I JUST HAD to move on ..." Yet, midway through the poem, when the narrator — Meta and all the women she evokes — elucidates the term "get it" as an inversion of for/get/it, she asks us to contemplate how suppressing the blues / rage forces us to demand the impossible like "make metal from flesh," calling to mind the history of Black women's bodies as reproductive machines, fodder, non-human, and superhuman. The realization of this impossibility calls her back to who she is and to find the strength to stop, breathe, and *choose* to not get it together or to forget it (whatever it is).

What does a word medicine woman do with all this? She writes herself whole. *Blues Doul*a is ritualistically designed: homage to the ancestors and elders (from Aretha Franklin to Aunt Elaine); emote and release for herself and the tribulations survived; and home, drawing on homage to and emotion in the quest to discover, claim, and stay home in oneself, community, and the world as a Black woman. It is in this last section that Meta Word Medicine Woman transforms into grand and authentic, never once ashamed of her scars, ever proud of what she is becoming and has become. In the end, *Blues Doula* is an exploration and revelation of what it means to take the journey towards living fully and free within oneself. It is a teaching, one that is offered to us as a gift of love.

—Maria Hamilton Abegunde
Indiana University, Bloomington

INTRODUCTION

My great grandmother introduced me to poetry while doing my hair and feeding me. My elder Chicago black poets, including my mother, built upon that foundation. Encouraging teachers and mentors had me write until I learned to extract a personal medicine from my words, in the way of my ancestors. Writing offered me voice in the day of Black Girl silencing. Poetry writing became spiritual practice and self-love. Now, I regularly stop to enjoy its flow.

    I lift my voice with Chicago-style honesty. I name my Black experience as in the feminine wound, father loss, family violence, environmental destruction, internalized racism, racial hatred and violence, and the overarching, paradoxical social role of today's Black woman. To come of age in the time of post-war boom is to be tempted by distraction of every sort, is to learn to walk, fly and die in the same, recurring moment. An exercise in revelation, in grieving while growing, accepting losses great and small to prepare again for what is real, next, these poems represent that stage of elder acceptance and relief.

    I wrap up this work anticipating another fine chapter!

— M.C.

ONE
HOMAGE

Coretta

I saw
her grace,
special, humble
holding
history's grapes
and
then
squeezing, squeezing, squeezing
until her skin soaked the juices
until Time stopped
in her hair
in her backbone
as all else round about her
withered.

Saw her
im/mort/al/ize tragedy
teaching us
his memory
meth/od/i/cal
planting seeds
1, 2, 3, A, B, C,
teaching us
to know
his cadence,
his wordsounds,
his brightest thoughts,
the ways of his feet —

to say his name
with that southern lilt
and remember ...

Saw her making sure
taking care
insisting, claiming
his place
at Legacy's Table reserved,
making sure,
raising
her head, her children,
answering critics
un/flap/pa/ble,
ever
forever planting
1, 2, 3, A, B, C
for the rest of her days
im/a/gin/ing
cul/tiv/at/ing,
harvesting
an honor crop.

Saw her creating
a regal thing
from the bloodsoaked
spoils of struggle —
her Destiny
his Legacy,
a regal thing

by hand
in the way
of her people
a regal thing
I saw her ...
ever
forever
Queen.

Cissy's 2012 Poem

Sometimes all a prophet can do
is describe what looms,
prepare for great dawnings
whisper prayers
into hands rubbed bare
and wait...

Then, once time had come and gone
time to unclench numerous
fisted, fixed, forced notions
the Hands of Time
snatched the Last Petal
from our rarest Princess Flower,
that one cultivated & groomed
at the queens' knees.

Ah, but the queens could
only impart regal tradition,
known melodious beauty
rooted, grounded, beyond question
that natural inheritance,
she became and gave
by heart.

"*Doesn't* she know?"
I asked the howling, frozen winds...
watching her sidestep herself
turn silently
morph, veer farther still —

in search of another something
another thrilling comfort
familiar, yet mystical.

"Didn't she *know*?"
short memory demanded.
When in truth, this sadness
grew gradual, lengthy —
her echo chamber narrowed, collapsed,
fast forwarded,
visible, palpable agony
ex/a/cer/bat/ing
their glacial mockery, ridicule, plucking,
her desire
feasting on time and skin.

Unbeknownst still,
vast air and sky gushed from her mouth
her star shone far beyond brilliance
propelled by dream frequencies
able to shatter difference
and pierce all hearts
with audible whelm,
with extra celestial
love.

Perhaps now,
at last departure
in restful stillness
taken like strong medicine
at evening's end

her last whisper faded,
question answered,
pain quieted,
perhaps now, at last
and forever
She knows.

Two Seconds Tender
(for Burt Bacharach)

Curious composer's anatomy
curved neck, shoulders, back
citing, marking
from whence his lessons come.
He whispers wails,
uncanny, agile —
Ray Charles' generation
tipping that
Steinway bench.

Bringer of wind chimes
musical time passages
overflow from his pockets,
spill wise everywhere he goes —
complete messages suspended
in the ethers —
ripe fruit
hanging heavy
from the limb.

Muted trumpet surrogate voice
piano tears punctuate,
break open old
stagnant head places
with insistent love —
love's conundrum,
love's questions

crying on strings
crying out for more
of love's self.
Eloquent, even, especially,
when love has died.

Awe, this tender truth
and graceful greatness,
hopeful, humble,
profuse, keyboard love
offered precise peace,
conducted, commanded couplets
folded, stirred into medleys,
transformed two hours
into two breathtaking
seconds.

We whose lives he
lubricated, warmed and moved,
with stacatto,
hard times specials —
reopened constricted heart spaces
returned these prodigal feet
to destined paths —
We lived his themes,
rode his rising chords,
his heavy winds, rapid melodies
carried us,
beyond unspoken beyonds...

We, his boomer contingent
gray beards and heads
bowed, wept,
as he walked us back
back, back
across memory's horizon
with
that easy orange-pink
soundtrack.

Yes, we relived
an incorrect
then corrected
dynamic with ourselves
as we listened
and we melted
again
each time
he
sang...

Aretha

Our complete sentence.
Beyond music,
she voiced
our truth
for the time capsule.
Call me the moment
the second...
Our giant redwood
Remember this house!
it reached
so long, so long
for golden skies —
Our giant redwood
felled
tumbled
flattened a straight
new path extended
adorned,
soaked with melody
harmony, rhythm
her new di/men/sion/al
purity, legacy
royalty
oh me, oh my!
So far sighted —
she peered beyond
her neighborhood chances
looked instead
to the highest hills,

to those cosmic, galactic
prophetic hills
of ALL possibilities
& took her rightful
place
in the heavenly choir.
She gifted us
angelic
sound
uplifted
echoed
af/fir/mat/ive sound.

Reverend Re Re
preached the gospels
of *Amazing Grace,*
Doctor Feelgood,
R-e-s-p-e-c-t
Just a little bit!
Reverend Re Re
re-framed
re-tooled
re-imagined
their aria, their songs,
young, gifted & black,
then gave them back
better
bolder
driving *a Pink Cadillac*
breathing a Grown

Natural Woman's
breath
a Grown
Natural Woman's
ver/nac/u/lars
day-dream-ing
from her heart, her life.
Aretha
filled her time
past the brim
spilled herself
beyond music —
I'm only One Step away…
I'm Eleanor Rigby
in a
Chain, Chain, Chain.
She voiced
our truth,
all the lonely people
& she
now…
sounds…
off…
day-dream-ing…
ex-hal-ing…
Aretha
hushed…
our
sentence
complete.

When We Dance ... (for Sting)

Flowing cello,
walking upright bass
& hushed harmonic vocals
softly conspire
to declare
a deeper love
disclosed
& bare skinned
while
the black bassist
blushes,
disbelieves.
He stands
stunned
in the face,
the sound,
and public display
of *love like that!*
Love
unabashed,
Grown Folks' love
promising
telling
conjuring
a Dream through living lyric
luring her
with a living alluring lyric
a Dream

involving heaven
&
angels wings
& dancing
the kind of
Dance one
gets to do
in this life
but
once.

Mama Frank

Mostly
she sauntered
that ever elegant
sidewalk two-step
disguising
the tired
before my eight-year-old
eyes.
Not until today
after she'd
been gone so long
from here
that her strong memory
shows up
in my ideas,
etched on my face
in my hair,
in the things I
don't, but need to say
surprises I miss
empty spaces
left open
before God,
in
The Change, ever present,
in the half bend of my knee,
jokes I don't get
yes,

in the steady
passage of time
that until today
had been
kept
locked down
and
quiet.

The Secret (for Aunt Elaine)

Gone.
Her
dreams,
torment,
thought goblins
mind bandits
es/carp/ment
all.
To remember her
is to shake
in the cold winds of her leaving —
shake in the temperature
of each happening
constant falling,
& rising so very far.
To feel the quickenings
of regret —
pressed against the
un/for/give/a/bles
handed down, so
thick, numerous,
the seeming walls
that choked the words
& locked the secrets up.

Love knows no secrets
or walls or goblins
not really.

& I stand calling for
the day when they all —
each per/ni/cious illusion,
shadow of shame
drop of false belief —
sink into the ground,
become the corpse we
cover with soil.

She's gone
Auntie who taught me
to dance the Funky Four Corners
so smooth & easy
she who wore her bronze mask
during the '68 riots
& wrapped in African garb declared,
"but, I'm *a soul* sister, Honey,
a soul sister!"
Her heartfelt
life-or-death
prophetic pleadings...
"Ooooooooo, he's handsome,"
warned her paused, pursed lips,
warned behind lifted brows
so that I'd know, & heed.

Touching, contacting next worlds
seeing, piercing through pretense
aching, pleading, writhing,
changing, shifting, taking the air,

the plunge, drifting, hurrying
toward any promised relief
& un/der/stand/ing —
She was
& is now
our Ancestor journeying on
journeying still
into the waiting arms of love
that knows no bounds,
time, pain,
se/pa/ra/tion.
Love that only knows
who She is.

Oh how I will miss her
genuine being
fever-pitch begging
just one ear
from deep inside
a hole locked
dis/lo/cat/ed, just one ear
for the healing,
& the truth is
I *always* missed her —
she was always missing
always hidden, loudly,
deeply hidden in plain view
& just missing...
Oh! How I will miss her!

Two
Emote

Ode to Brown Baby

Born dry,
old,
sliding Home safe
in an empty stadium.
Looking left, then right
looking heartbreak
square in the eye.
Looking to be sure,
dark rimmed ears
cupie curly
pug nosed curious
propped up, stuffed into one corner
of the prickly brown sofa.
Propped beside
the ones with plastic skin
propped before
she could sit up
or hold her head up,
propped and bobbing.
Born fat, believing
looking beyond baby days —
tiny, triumphant
deep down brown creation song
in a marigold's face.
Stooped over
beneath the weight of that
sad soundtrack
and piano music
she learned early.

Two-times-five
multiplied time
pushing past
forgotten stick-around brown
Daddy's baby brown
shakin' in the words
her forgotten brown words
finger poppin' slaphappy words
and stories.
'Til they took
that brown baby
to be baptized words
to be saved words
to the church house words
where Jesus lived
since He sure didn't live
where the peaches grew.
'Til they hushed her
tellin' teachin' her
of that war
where soldiers
and guns were just invisible.
Where's that brown baby
left-behind brown
in the peaches
in the cream?
At its core,
one-by-one love
not both or all love
just ahead of wind gusts
love in a flood

brown baby talk words,
to see, know, remember
reflect, more time multiplied
over quilted make-do struggle
understand scrambled, smothered
need beggin' sound
with the wise ones' help.
Believin' in Vick's salve
and rubbin' alcohol
in golden triumphant brown,
to stop the war on brown
brown love brown beauty
goodness, peace and mercy
ever dreamin' 'bout
that finger pressin' the bell
that one, determined brown finger
pressin' real hard
on that bell.
Dreamin' hearin' that bell
That is —
'til her backbone formed
her eyes beheld her own
beauty brown dawning new
right now new
knowin' she hadn't missed out
not really,
knowin' in her tiny graspin'
brown hand
there was already
always a way to sit straight,
to touch the root reasons,

to see her
long-haired kittens
playin' in the tulip gardens
to hear her whisperin' sunshine
to taste her jumbo ripe blackberries
fillin' her up
and have everything else
she loves
right there
as she
watches, smiles,
as she
stands up
and
walks.

'71 Love Poem

Once, on the nuptial's eve,
I imagined love
was black leather,
blurred beautiful behind cigarette smoke
fragrant black leather
loosely wrapped against the cold,
wrapped around Ellie's theme...
her sweet, soulful wishes
sweaty, lifegiving smooth,
warm black skin
that never spoke,
words never found,
words never expected.

So,
he.
ain't.
said.
shit.
Not what he wanted,
not what he dreamed of
not who his Mama was,
if he had a cousin
an Auntie, or a Daddy.
Quick! Like second hands
he moved
to the beat
of his own
imagined theme,

moved, a whole m.o.
donned the coat, turtleneck,
shiny hair, packed and parted,
long legged walk, stance
cased the block,
carried a badge,
fed a shivering, hungry child
with a smile and a dollar bill.
Talked only
to the cats,
shoe shine parlor cats
precinct station cats,
Harlem street cats
Bumpy's cats
says all he must
with that small piece
of paper
before he stops again.

Pretty Ellie
kept the light on
for her black man.
Hers, she thought,
that one she let hold
her extra key.
Ready, running to his tallness
after he scuffed his shoes and
got to "feeling like a machine,
that's no way to feel…" he hinted…
Last on his list,
Pretty Ellie's

happy to be on it
at all.
Happy to be his.
Happy he's her only baby.
"I love you," she sang,
"I know,"
"take it easy..."
his half-hearted hang up...

Once, on the nuptial's eve
and with no theme at all
I imagined love was black,
any, every dark
shade of brown leather —
mink, fox, mahogany —
any dark shade of brown —
power, assuming.
Once, on the nuptial's eve
I imagined real
love was jet black,
silent swag
any dark darker
hip
slick
shade
of long
brown leather,
my sweet, silent
love...

Blues Doula

Today remember them
central
in the squeezing
loop
of this proving, lonely rage:
Yes. They would —
float up,
up, up from life's cellar —
my moldy, tainted tears
stifled
in shame over needs of my skin.
Most times I ignored
their urging,
ignored them speaking —
demanding emergence —
pushing their way out.
No! I swallowed
choked, fought them back
pretended they didn't exist.
What black woman tears?
So
I smiled instead,
denied them,
turned my back
on all of them,
on my own tears
and pressed ahead —
pressed
      pressed

because
I'd cried enough already,
TOO MUCH even,
because
I didn't need
more washing,
cleansing,
still more letting go
because
I JUST HAD to move on,
to for get about it
to for give it,
to get over it,
to get on with it,

to get it together
to get my mind made up.
To get, get, get, get,
get it on,
get it right,
get it straight,
get real,
get ahead,
get the page turned,
get the chapter closed,
get thicker skin now,
get it sucked up,
get it — take care of business,
get it — make metal from flesh,
get this mountain climbed
       with second hand child's gear,

climb this mountain
    whether I know how or not
climb it, just hold steady and climb —
up
    hold our tradition
and multi
    task
up
    hold super images.
    But wait!
Nobody told me I'd be climbing!
Climbing,
crying —
scaling new heights
through spilling tears
scaling new heights,
everything liquefying,
running together...
So... I... stop today...
soak up the voices, the gushes
with my palms.
For I
can't climb and cry,
can't climb and cry, will not,
won't soldier, climb,
cry,
and get it
together...
today.

Intersection

In this place
where converging forces
dan/ger/ous/ly
dare me
where noises blare,
deafen
& life's speed
dizzies
where traffic crawls,
I stand
barefoot
upon cold, broken
harshness,
& lean, bend quickly
this way & that,
jump aside
to avoid
steel on skin.

In this place
I stand naked,
ignored
nav/i/gat/ing
this inched space
as you see me
barely, through blinders
merely, coveting,
ro/man/tic/iz/ing,
coveting
my voice
my love
& my milk,

expecting me
to soothe
& distract
you,
to teach you
to feel
implore you
to tell your
truth
while you
mimick
mine,
while you
ap/pro/pri/ate
my cries, longings,
caring not
one iota,
not one damned bit
that this is MY
medicine,
caring not
that this is how
I stayed alive
not caring
that this death defying
dance is
what kept
me here
— where converging
dangerous forces
kept time …
for us
both.

Umbilicus

But we were young
together,
my first love
our delicate sisterhood.
So I looked way up
to where she was,
for all I wanted
was long hair,
that twinkling smile
& the deep dimples
like she had.
To be able
to say things
that way,
& get
what I wanted
like she did.
But, the stiff Rule Book
was
clear:
only one of us
would speak
at a time.

Young together,
and when
my boyfriends
saw *her,*
well…

there wasn't much
else to be seen.
So, we tried not
to bump heads
until much later...
when my wedding
dress found her
jealous
for one of her own.

Several moon seasons
and much living
later
I felt her
slam on brakes!
Screeching, she stopped it all —
of a sudden
the wanting
dreaming, planning
getting, having.

From here she would coast only,
reverse magic
forfeit beauty
forget the way:
her dried peonies
now pressed in a faded scrapbook.
Old, remaining years racing forward
like a cartoon clock.
Circling back to birth status
after so many departures,

leaving tread marks,
with nothing more
to be
but holy —
learning to lean
I'm learning to lean.

I stand in this crater
decorated simply
by her heart shards —
fearing nothing
so much
as the sound of her
words growing few
tight
small
faint,
as the sights
& feel of her life
our delicate sisterhood
e/vap/or/at/ing
before me,
as she,
silently, desperately
expects me…
like always
to
o/be/di/ent/ly
follow…
along.

Lament: Ode to Mother Emmanuel

Ancient emotion leaks
from my marrow,
from all around the Circle of Life,
ancient emotion now uncontained,
respirating, circulating, undulating
erupting, spilling, spinning, striving,
sputtering, splashing
wherever it can
everywhere it falls,
to the nearest places
splattering, covering, coloring, carrying life with it
evidence of life,
contents under pressure,
under siege
exploding, running easily downward, draining,
drifting,
dropping south, seeking its lowest, most likely home.

And so, I grieve all our losses, lives, land, broken
spaces, stolen dreams,
grieve the nightmarish toil
our ancestors endured together,
morphing, and from so doing,
becoming One People.
I grieve with tears so long denied,
crying out loud,
my pores allowing it,
finally agreeing
and letting the loosed fire, water, air, earth and sky

escape,
trapped, silenced, muted, masked, mumbled,
murmured, muzzled
no more.

And at last I fully weep,
writhe, wrestle, scream
the endless assaults,
atrocities, absurdities,
ap/pro/pri/a/tion
of all that we are/have/had
and, after these tears dry,
I collect, claim, collage
the shards,
parts and pieces of us,
then,
on behalf of us all,
I ask you ...
bone of my bone,
flesh of my flesh ...
What, what, what
whatever,
what more
what in the hell
what is it
what in this world
what the fuck
WHAT
DO
YOU
WANT???

Dark, Darker, Darkest

… Isn't just skin color
or the million
miniature
rainbows dancing
down sunrays
glowing off Onyx's
ebony coat.

It's the spectrum
of a lifetime's
emotion shunned,
denied, translated,
vacuum packed
and flash pasteurized.

It's seasons of power
sudden awareness
of every imagined
urgent
emphatic cussword
left on the tongue
unuttered.

It's the memory
of every tasted
escapist concoction
yearned for,
or some dangerous

trist in my skin, oh no,
never risked.

It's bartering my
self for salvation.
Insulating, wrapping up
in make-believe,
protecting against this
cold, menacing construct a/k/a
whiteness.

Double Consciousness

Humanity's lamb
I am
suckler & starved
lover & despised
artist & paint
primary colors
sought after soul
creosote woman
super/natural strength
incredible hulk & eternal martyr
complete with
spiritual hook-up ...
I swear
I can get a prayer through.

I am poet & poem
writer most written
pen in worn out hand
seeking well lit words
words broken open
word pearls
word jewels
word diamonds
awaiting discovery
speak my truth
if you dare

Speak my truth
& live
my flood,
tears,
sweat, blood
spilled on soil — tears
for without me
there is drought,
without us
drought is certain
& without us
you
die of thirst
too.

Say My Name

My midnight taunts, ter/ror/i/zes
your dreams where I
snatch your roots
send you hurrying
sur/rend/er/ing
your in/her/it/ance
at the nearest Poor Man's Bank;
where I keep you
forgetting, breathless,
entranced by Bigger, Better and More
then, when all else fails,
I've got you
taking one another.

My printed smiles
mask your pain
in that corporate brothel
you say you hate
where my purpose paints every face,
drives distrusting debate
where biweekly, my numeric image
quickly meets your palm
and sedates you
that much more.

Standing between you
and all that
you fear, I am
your relief, pac/i/fi/er.

You cannot get enough of me
no, never an overdose
for I alone permit —
I am the traffic signal
for all your Big Decisions.

Say my name.

I alone decide
what's worthwhile.
When I am away,
you are paralyzed, thirsty, famished,
you say you have failed,
your ca/pa/ci/ties cancelled
for with me,
you're well,
made whole in the face of loss,
made safe, strong, victorious
after injury.

It is my reflection
in your mirror,
your scowls and smiles all mine!
Most times I define "re/spon/si/ble,"
"practical" "wealth," "beauty"
right where you live.
Do you give?

It is my up-tone inflection
in your voice, your impetus
the trendy chic of all you want.
Code words disguise my face —
and you'll even abandon learning
preferring me, if you think I'm nearby!
You will postpone your health
and your love
for me.

I overtook the land,
killed your mind with fanciful flesh,
sleek gadgets, weapons, colorful castles,
pastries and noises
made pleasant to your palate.
Now, for me,
you kill the land
your brother, yourself,
all you said was good
for you hate that plain old,
undone life without me.

I said say it!
Say my name,
just once.
Right where you live
Do you give?

Soil Sorrows

Anchored, broad, tight,
giant gnarled fists clenching soil
with circles etched in endless palms
a thousand rings stitched fine and close
for miles they reached past rooftops
strong, skyward
their hair flowing thick,
filtering sunbeams,
permitting bits of icy wind
blowing strong
past my windows
up my nostrils
as we shared connected spaces,
coalesced nicely yet unaware.
They blocked the wintry bite.
Many days, we quickly came and went.
Many mornings their claws offered cushion
for sharpening tinier ones
their base brimming with sap,
a reason for hope
a basin for rains
of every color..

These greenswaying
grandmother umbrellas
let but few drops through,
stood content, stretched over,
covered everyone safely beneath.
Their great trunks a daybreak home

for birdsongs and squirrels play
their trunks, massive evening ears
stretching branches a dusktime home
to raccoon babies' balled up bodies
bouncing limb to limb,
leaning posts for the forgotten, the broken,
touchstones when small stuff grew big —
Until suddenly machines came,
grinding, buzzing,
white cranes and ramps conspiring
pulling, scraping, ripping, drilling, cracking
their lifeline, causing screams
to crumble/tumble into pieces,
stacked and shaved of green
thrown onto a slick, extra-long flatbed
branching arms shoved
into the shredding tube,
dying dust spewed out the other end.

I pass the cold holes where my
generous friends once stood,
feel their spirit hover as wind and light
now beat my crown.
I hear their mournful screams
the tearing of skin and hair
done to union cadence, in phases
until moments expired,
crew stopped and left —
them stumped, balded,
severed, scattered
gashed in disbelief, laid still

on the ground
until their return —
to prepare the way,
perhaps
for a chic new patio.

Now those they sheltered
shrug off, move about seeming
not to mourn the old lives
just ground to dust
long lives ann/i/hil/at/ed,
in two short days
lives giving life
lives grown gradually,
over a century
of love, light, rainstorms
their stories to become.

While those on two legs
whom they nourished
come to gawk, rush
roundabout their demise
pretend not to mind,
as those much wiser —
those on four and winged
scamper, scurry, squawk confused
displaced, wondered, sought the day
of peace under foot
when
nightmarish

Earth
Mother killing
for money and style
is
at last obsolete,
at last wicked,
at last
an/thro/po/cene.

Madagascar

Her colorful myth
told of a man
damn near white —
a man devoid of slavery
a man, they say, whose people
came from Africa's
OTHER side.

Her myth recalled
that silenced mother
this father of thirteen
this masonry man,
who built his home of stones by hand
his name
inscribed on their
little Dry Town's charter.

Beloved father
she said,
his baby daughter's birth
a total surprise.
As quickly
he lost another daughter
to the cold creek waters
where she jumped
to stop the blood.
And his baby granddaughter
refused his funeral?

She thought
they needed her homespun heroic myths
to cover the questions rising,
questions of how his clever people
fled north to Canada,
where they stayed
until Emancipation.

Of how this Madagascar clan
devoid of slavery
used brown Madagascar paper
to protect
their Madagascar
plantation eyes, hair, and skin
color line.

Of how this landless mountaineer clan
devoid of slavery
named itself anew,
lived in a papery stick house
whupped their babies,
put them to sleep
and
did it
to their daughters
all times of day and night
just like ole massa —
shoved, blew them through
the Door of Confidence
and into early graves
then sought by every means
to distinguish,

to distance
its Madagascar self
from black —
from the rest of
them niggas
over there ...
per
    man
        ent
            ly.

THREE
HOME

Crone Song

Push
Press —
Today's cool russet,
golden, lime
and cranberry
deliver me up
to slow
motion
where I circle
settle into
this easier rhythm
that song
set long
before I really noticed
and I ... am still noticing —

Slow motion
where the yearning,
syrupy juices
of my life
simply want
to marinate
simmer,
thicken, sweeten
make wine forever
as I dream a new dream.

Push
press a poem past
whatever the
clock insists...
still I squeeze
all remaining life
from the pulp,
suck and lap
it up,
ahhhhhhhhhh,
to assure
my daughter
that yes,
she, too, can do
this thing her way,
she can do it however
she pleases.

One (for Mama)

"Hear, O Israel,
the Lord, our God, is One"
She says again,
and I smile.
"Every breath
from His hand…"
she reminds
"Yes, Ma'am,"
I nod, for the day
of resistance is past.
One breath. Hear.

She teaches simply
of days when
we breathed fully
for each other…
She for me
as I set out blind,
down a one-way road
invisible beyond my feet
a road, winding, circular
steep, arduous, flooded,
thankless, long,
but
beautiful.
She for me. Ruth.

I for her
when windy decisions
shifted suddenly
and temperatures plunged
below freezing,
falling
mute where stories
would have been
falling
empty where others once were
falling
bare inside this little closet
with only sky for ceiling,
one hand-held candlelight,
one exit bolted
us two together,
lavender fragrance diffusing
the air between us.
One.
I for her. Mary.

"Hear, O Israel,
the Lord, our God, is One"
One.
Reduced, abased,
subtracted, skinned,
scraped
of dross, trappings, excess,
One.

"Every breath
from His hand..."
she insists again.

"Yes, Ma'am," I answer,
my head bowed,
slowly wondering
what wisdom I'll speak
into
my daughter's spirit —
what grace or gratitude
freedom or forgiveness —
when it comes my time
to fly...
One.

Hair

Time and peoples
banded stranded
silver, off-black, sable
crawl, seek, latch,
wave, curl, knot, string.
Finger twisted freedom
grows wild
along existing circles
tightens, slowly locks
lengthens simple
from
baby curls to cloth
framed nub-ettes
to thriving
long and longer tassels
for playful
sometimes joyous tosses,
jeweled crowns, chopsticks, rolls,
a house for incense,
multiple Nubian glories.

So satisfied
to co/op/er/ate,
ap/pre/ci/ate
what is
more than enough,
what is
so happily moist,
substantial,

what is
wonderfully thick
and covering,
I smile, sing
at long last
of glad connection
of a love affair
with
my
hair.

Mama

From silent word well
empty shell
abandoned cell
returns this soul

searching precise
unsaid ways to say
or best describe
spirit mother

tough leather coated
facing gusts and
torrents sure
harmonic blessings
uttered pure

resilient, steady, cooled
pressing against ages
ever loving
peace warrior

calling cantaloupe
rhubarb gardens
back into view
weaving beauty here

homemade candy
her wisest ways
her feet step light
that the blind may see

what life her eyes have seen
dreams her heart believed
lessons her fingers sculpted
out of dust and smoke

meals her hands prepared
prayers her lips spoke
hugs her arms squeezed
slights her heart forgave

coats she made,
tough
double-lined secure
mother, found

just mother
deeply rooted,
our mountainside tree,
blown, stretched skyward

laughing, living
far enough away
from raging currents
to stay dry

just mother
calling cantaloupe
rhubarb gardens
back into view
birthing, weaving beauty
here

Genesis Three Sixteen

Cool harvest moon's
glowing shadows usher in
forbidden memory —
Genesis 3:16 —
culminates
ac/cen/tu/ates
Change, on the earth's axis,
that I am o/bli/vi/ous
no more.
My mother was god,
Black Poet
finding
oh so rare and
perfect words
for
love and nightmares,
so few
that it behooved me
to study, to know well
her darkest midnight
and forbidden
ripe red.

Secretly
with one eye open
I watched
god turn herself
inside out

and count,
count it joy,
heard her secret
whimpers cry in rhythm
to the
squeaky springs,
wondered how much it hurt
and why still
she was
his cushion
from the weight
of life.

With both eyes open
I sought to trust, emulate,
covet, confide in
hear, empathize with, follow
her,
as danger
became
destiny
death, swallowing
her lovers
like Jonah's whale,
swallowing —
like she always longed to —
devour,
consume
the forbidden ripe red.

Wondering how
her softness
survived
a mandated maiden trilogy:
Virginity, (or reasons),
Beauty, (or make-up),
Baptism ... or else.
Wondering how
she survived the soilings —
pretty pink moon soiled cloth
forbidden ripe red soiled
spilled and spilling more.

Not recognizing,
yet ever
wondering
about the
most important things
that god
just
never, ever
mentioned.
Forever I watched her
swallow, absorb, survive
the life she craved.
Watched, studied her so I would be
o/bli/vi/ous
no
more.

What I Miss

I: Analog Life
in first person present tense
FLESH time
ask somebody,
an actual human being time
abundant human contact time
shoe leather
sanity time
REAL options time
AFFORDABLE food time
together MEAL time
the Juice Man
tiny, hand painted juice glass time.
TRUST time.
Handwritten note from home
a quarter pack of cigarettes
corner grocery store time.
Mama Frank's
Lipton tea and sugar toast breakfast time.
Her healing hands time.
My mother.
My brother.
TV time.
Real smiles and belly laughs time.
Carrying on time.
RESPECT understood time.
Knowing when to say WHEN time.
Time enough to recognize
hypnosis and DECIDE time.

Sewing slowly in the SILENCE time.
Living well with very little time
Thick, nighttime MUSIC
from crickets time
Animals time,
Honeybees and fresh air time.
Wild mustard and milkweed pods
growing beside the train tracks time
Diver Dan and the Barracuda.
American Bandstand time.
Strolling to New Orleans
with Fats Domino time.
Test pattern on a silent screen
after bedtime ...
Time. Remember the time?
Shutting, locking the front door
EVERY night to
leave the world outside time.

II: Analog friendship and love
silly, spontaneous, available
no appointment necessary time:
"Girl, did you see Bewitched?"
Telephone boyfriend,
first kiss back porch full moon time.
Blushing.
Love songs with innuendo. Time.
Cute boy carrying my books,
breathless swooning. Time.
LAUGH until I cried time.
Learn latest dances on playground.

Double Dutch, always good times.
Encouraging sisterhood good Time.

III: Analog school
Joe Cobb's
great get-up morning JAMS.
Walk to school time.
Transistor radios.
Red and blue mailbox at the corner time.
Sack lunches.
Real teaching. Time.
Arithmetic We Need.
Childish thinking, imagining, conjuring
practical joking time.
Music class.
Art class.
Figure things out time.
Pencil sharpening time,
believing knives were deadliest time.
Motor Town soundtrack
for it all time, not knowing our music was forever
time.
One Boogie Man at a time. Time.
The right to my dreams time.
Short sleeved blouses with
Peter Pan collars time.
Polished white gym shoes and
passing inspection time.
Saturday night bath time.

IV. Analog church
clapping, dancing, shouting time.
Pass the fan with the praying hands time.
Carson Pirie Scott & Co.
Charles A. Stevens & Co.
Patent leather church shoes ... on sale time.
Weekly special occasion time
to look and feel my best. Time.
Singing time. Marching in time.
Praying time. Crying time. Hands holding time.
Mother's Day, Easter Sunday and
our church anniversary time.
Sweet potato pie, collard greens and cornbread
when water was free
and POP was a dime. Time.

Our little house that leaned to the side. Time.
the look, sound and feel of
my Selectric typewriter time.
And every now and then,
catch my breath and
BLAM,
that satisfying SLAM time
receiver to cradle
on my black,
steel,
built-to-last
TELEPHONE
time.

Black Echoes

To be black
is to see
the whole human imprint
and to bear its mark
on your mind flesh

To be black
is to live vigilant
work for change
make your ancestors' music
all while you sleep

To be black
is to know
the truth you've lived
and remain hopeful
especially
when hope makes no sense

To be black
is to know
full well what time it is
and still decide
to wait in that long line
for the dance

To be black
is to douse the flames

of your pride
constantly,
and to invent new ways
to look hatred in the face
for your child's sake

To be black
is to love
with your whole self
and not miss the chance
to find, take back,
polish and reset
every lost piece
that they stole from you

To be black
is to grow sure, wide-eyed,
cradled
in the lap of history
and to know
that your every breath
is prophetic

To be black
is to understand that your life
was, is and will be
good enough
to hold all of it
together … while you take flight.

ABOUT THE AUTHOR

Born into a family of artists where writing of all kinds took place, Meta Commerse, Word Medicine Woman, teaches, writes, heals and performs her generative words. *Blues Doula* is her second poetry collection, the first, *Rainsongs: Poems of a Woman's Life*, (2012). Meta earned her MFA in Creative Writing at Goddard College. She's the author of *The Mending Time* (2014), her story medicine novel, of *Womaning, a Memoir* (forthcoming) and of *Diamonds and Pyramids: Story Medicine for Racial Healing* (forthcoming). She is founder of Story Medicine Worldwide based in Western North Carolina where she lives, teaches courses and designs healing excursions using this Indigenous modality. She's the mother of three adult children and grandmother to three young adult grandsons living in Georgia.

www.ingramcontent.com/pod-product-compliance
Lightning Source LLC
Chambersburg PA
CBHW071412290426
44108CB00014B/1797